John Stuart Ogilvie

Seven hundred album verses

Choice selections of poetry and prose

John Stuart Ogilvie

Seven hundred album verses
Choice selections of poetry and prose

ISBN/EAN: 9783741192081

Manufactured in Europe, USA, Canada, Australia, Japa

Cover: Foto ©Andreas Hilbeck / pixelio.de

Manufactured and distributed by brebook publishing software (www.brebook.com)

John Stuart Ogilvie

Seven hundred album verses

COMPRISING

OICE SELECTIONS OF POETR AND PROSE,

SUITABLE FOR WRITING IN AUTOGRAPH ALBUMS,

AND FOR

NTINES, BIRTHDAY, CHRISTMAS AND NEW YE/ CARDS.

ORIGINAL ECTED.

Our lives are a through,
With good or ill, false or true,
as the blessed angels turn the pages of our years,
grant that they may read the good with smiles,
And blot the ill with tears.

By

WHO among the readers of this pr[eface] ce has not been invited to write a fe[w w]ords of sentiment in the album of [a fr]iend? As an aid to the many tho[usa]nds who have received this invitatio[n a]nd have not known what to write, v[e of]fer this collection of choice verse a[nd pr]ose, as an aid to them and all othe[rs w]ith the hope that our labor shall n[ot h]ave been spent in vain, nor be alt[oge]ther unappreciated. Great care h[as b]een taken to procure as many *origin[al p]ieces* as possible. Many choice vers[es su]itable for Birthday, Christmas a[nd N]ew Year celebrations, have bee[n ad]ded; which, with the collection [of ar]ticles embracing sentiment, affectio[n, h]umor, and miscellany, is offered to [a g]enerous public by

EDICATION VERSES, - - -
NTIMENT AND AFFECTION,
ISCELLANEOUS, - - - -
STEEM AND CONFIDENCE, -
UMOROUS, - - - - -
RTHDAY VERSES, - - - -

[SU]ITABLE FOR INSCRIPTION ON TITLE PAGES [OF] ALBUMS.

[W]ithin this book ne'er may there ste[al]
    thought to make a fair one feel
    single pang of heartfelt grief,
[O]r slightest sorrow, e'er so brief;
[B]ut let each line the muse inspires
[B]e filled with ardent, pure desires,
[T]hat every good on thee may rest,
[A]nd every blessing be possessed,
[W]hate'er we ask for those we love,
[F]rom earth below or heaven above.
[M]ay ne'er the sigh of anguish blast
[O]ne bright memorial of the past;
[O]r wavering doubt, or anxious fear,
[B]e caused by aught recorded here.
[Y]et warm affection, pure and bright,
[C]ast o'er each page its hallowed ligh[t]
[T]hus may this album ever be
[F]rom vice, and pride, and passion fre[e]
[F]rom every grosser taint refined,
[A]n emblem of the stainless mind;
[A]nd though thy friends afar may be
[B]eyond the wide, wide rolling sea—
[O], think not they will e'er forget

As you have conferred on me t
vor of dedicating your album, I f(
yself under renewed obligation
esent you a memento of respect a
teem.

May you find many true friends w
ill interest themselves in your beh
id leave an expression of their atta(
ent to you in this book—a token th
all endure when widely separated
me and space.

Go, leafy compendium, and gath
veets from every flowery pen ; plur
y wings with richest gems, nor p(
it thy pages to become contaminat
y poisonous sentiments.

This is the earnest prayer of yc
worthy friend.

Go forth, thou little volume
I leave thee to thy fate ;
To love and friendship truly
Thy leaves I dedicate.

---

o, little book, thy destined cou
   pursue,
ollect memorials of the just and tr
nd beg of every friend so near

When years elapse,
It may, perhaps,
Delight us to review these scraps
And live again 'mid scenes so gay,
That time's rough hand has swept away
Or when the eye, bedimmed with age
Shall rest upon each treasured page,
Those pleasant hours
That once were ours
Shall come again, like autumn flowers,
To bloom and smile upon us here
When all things else seem sad and drear
Will tune our hearts and make them sing,
And turn our autumn into spring!

As life flows on from day to day,
And this, your book, soon fills,
How many may be far away
From treasured vales and hills?
But there is joy in future time
To turn the pages o'er,
And see within a name or rhyme
From one you'll see no more.

Go forth, thou little volume,
Like Noah's faithful dove,
And bring to darling ———

My album's open! Come and see!
What! Won't you waste a line on me
Write but a thought, a word or two,
That memory may revert to you.

———

Go, album! range the gay parterre;
  From gem to gem, from flower
    flower.
Select with taste and cull with care,
And bring your offering, fresh and rare
  To this sweet maiden's bower!

———

TO MY FRIENDS:
My album is a garden spot
  Where all my friends may sow,
Where thorns and thistles flourish not
  But flowers alone may grow.
With smiles for sunshine, tears for
    showers,
I'll water, watch and guard these flowers

———

Life is a volume,
  From youth to old age,
Each year forms a chapter,
  Each day is a page.
May none be more charming,
  More womanly (manly) true,
Than that, pure and noble,

[M]any kind wishes will be written he[re]
[A]nd none more sincere than mine.
[B]ut—
[W]ords are lighter than the cloud-fo[am]
  Of the restless ocean's spray;
[F]ainer than the trembling shadows
  That the next hour steals away.
[B]y the fall of summer raindrops
  Is the air as deeply stirred,
[A]nd the roseleaf that we tread on
  Will outlive a word.

———

[W]e may write our names in albums,
  We may trace them in the sand,
[W]e may chisel them in marble,
  With a firm and skillful hand;
[B]ut the pages soon are sullied,
  Soon each name will fade away;
[E]very monument will crumble,
  Like all earthly hopes, decay.
[B]ut, dear friend, there is an album,
  Full of leaves of snowy white,
[W]here no name is ever tarnished,
  But forever pure and bright.
[I]n that Book of Life, God's Album,
  May your name be penned with c[are]
[A]nd may all who do here write,

o little volume, like the bee,
 The fertile fields of mind explore,
ull from each mental shrub and tree
 Some *grateful* sweets to *swell* thy
  store.
o, and in friendship's hallowed name
 Where'ere thy wanderings may be,
 tribute fond from feeling claim,
 A few brief lines for *Memory*.

Go, little book. Bring the be ishes of happiness to the fair own this memorial of friendship; ar ather the brightest gems of Virtu steem and Love from the fairy fiel a bright future.

Fly, little volume, to the mount whe [ope's bright star ever glitters abo· 1e horizon and colors those flowers iendship that fade not; but, ev lled with the dews of affection, sca :rs its sweet influence around the pat ay of our dear friend when the lowe 1g clouds and storms of affliction hov er her dwelling to make her disco)late, and her home a place of sorro· hen wilt thou, as a soul cheerir

Album, who will greet thee with smiles, and shake thy dewy plumes of esteem, and spread before her those many gems that thou hast gathered from the fields of *Adieux.* May she not feel deserted and alone; but, surrounded by many friends that will ever wish her happiness and a pathway flower strewn.

CAST ON THE WORLD.

On friendship's realm thou art
Spotless, till now unsullied yet in part.
Go, little book, and on each page receive
The various offerings which true friends
    may give.
Ask not the crowd, but seek refinement's
    pen,
Wielded by virtue, that unerring gem.
Of parting friends some kind memorial
    keep,
Of those who part, perhaps no more to
    meet.

SENTIMENT AND AFFECTION

Peace be around thee, wherever thou rovest;
 May life be for thee one summer's day;
And all that thou wish, and all that thou lovest,
 Come smiling around thy summer way.
If sorrow e'er this calm should break,
 May even thy tears pass off so lightly,
Like spring showers, they will only make
 The smiles that follow shine more brightly.

May the chain of friendship formed by the links which are dropped here, serve to unite you more closely in spirit with the friends who have worked it.

May each link be brought to a white heat in the fires of Love; and, forged on the anvils of Truth, may they be strong as iron, yet light as air, keeping you bravely to the duties of Life. And when the chain of human bondage shall be broken, may they become flowers of eternal brightness in the gardens from whence cometh exceeding peace.

Our lives are albums written through
With good or ill—with false or true—
And, as the blessed angels turn
    The pages of our years,
God grant they read the good with
    smiles,
And blot the bad with tears.

Be a good girl and you will be a true woman.

May thy darkest hours in life be well lighted with the sunshine of contentment.

Yours sincerely—although merely—

How long we live, not years, but actions
    tell;
That man lives twice who lives the first
    life well.
Make then, while yet ye may, your
    God, your friend,
Whom Christians worship, yet not
    comprehend.
The trust that's given, guard; and to
    yourself be just;
For, live we how we can, yet die we
    must.

When the golden sun is setting,
  And your heart from care is free,
When o'er a thousand things you're thinking,
  Will you sometimes think of me?

Live well; how long or short, permit to heaven;
They who forgive most, shall be most forgiven.

Soar not too high to fall, but stoop to rise;
We masters grow of all that we despise.

Your fate is but the common fate of all;
Unmingled joys here to no man befall.

Though many flowers have faded from my life,
  And clouds obscure the brightness of its sky;
This have I learned: we can do much to make
  Our lives a blessing and our words a power,
If what we find to do, for Christ's dear sake,
  We do with faithfulness, from hour to hour.

It may occur in after life
That you, I trust, a happy wife,
Will former happy hours retrace,
Recall each well-remembered face.
At such a moment I but ask—
I hope 'twill be a pleasant task—
That you'll remember as a friend
One who'll prove true e'en to the end.

I saw two clouds at morning,
    Tinged by the morning sun,
And in the dawn they floated on
    And mingled into one;
I thought that morning cloud was blest,
It moved so sweetly to the west,
Such be your gentle motion,
Till life's last pulse shall beat,
And you float on in joy to meet
A calmer sea, where storms shall cease—
A purer sky, where all is peace.

When on this page you chance to look,
Just think of me and close the book.

These few lines to you are tendered,
    By a friend sincere and true;
Hoping but to be remembered
    When I'm far away from you.

Work, while yet the daylight shines,
  With a loving heart and true,
For golden years are fleeting by,
  And we are passing, too.

Wait not for to-morrow's sun
  To beam upon thy way,
For all that thou canst call thine own,
  Is in this *one to-day.*

Then learn to make the most of life—
  Make glad each passing day—
For time will never bring thee back
  The chances swept away.

Leave no tender word unsaid—
  Do good while life shall last ;—
You know the mill can never grind
  With the *water that is past.*

Let not the hours we've spent together,
  Go past as nothing by ;
Forget me not, e'en though you must
  Remember with a sigh.

We are all placed here to do something. It is for *us*, and not for *others*, to find out what that something is, and then, with all the energy of which we are capable, honestly and prayerfully to be about our business.

May the memories of your life be those which hands of love shall gild with pleasures of true friendship.

"Poor is the friendless master of a world. A world in purchase for a friend, is gain."

Let excellency of character, purity of mind, together with generous words and noble deeds, mark conspicuously your whole life, not omitting to learn to eat, in order that your physical powers may be strong and healthy; thereby strengthening and elevating the mental and intellectual.

I have tried for a week, and vainly I
    seek
Words of wisdom to write to you here;
So, wishing you life free from sorrow
    and strife,
Nor wanting in friends and good cheer,
With health—perhaps wealth—
    Love better than self,
And Truth, far the best, to the end;
    Since content it maintains
    While existence remains,
I subscribe myself, Truly, your friend.

In fair and sunny beauty, or gray 'neath
 evening skies,
The purple hills from misty vales up-
 ward to heaven rise:
Their rugged side we scarce can see
 o'er-decked with fern and heather,
That rings its scented violet bells
 through fair and stormy weather;
So may thy life be clothed with flowers,
 and breathe a purer air,
Fresh from the "everlasting hills,"
 knowing no grief or care,—
And if the sunny sky must pale, as pales
 the setting sun,
May it only show the stars are near,
 peeping out, one by one!

I would that I could express my mind
To you, dear friend, in scribbling some
 rhyme;
But you know my failing as well as I,
And you better get another to try.

  Oh! think of me some day
  When I am far away;
  I'll pray thy days be long
  And joyous as the song
  Of sweet birds singing near,
  Thy heart with love to cheer.

So slight a favor 'tis you crave,
    That I can scarce refuse compliance;
Nor shall I use the page you gave,
    To set your champions at defiance.

Dear lady, vainly awed, I praise
    That dimpled hand I pressed at parting;
Or those dark eyes, beneath whose gaze
    A cupid lurks equipped for darting.

Nor can I hope to lightly touch
    On charms so oft the theme of lovers;
To add another, while so much
    That beautiful about thee hovers.

I can but add one little pearl
    To all the gems about thee scattered;
And say again, sweet, artless girl,
    That all thy poets have not flattered.

I would not blot this page, but I would like to make a spot large enough to hold you to remembrance of your friend.

Thanksgiving-day again is here,
    And turkey is the leading question;
I wish, with heartiness sincere,
    That you may have a good digestion.

May joy thy spirit fill,
  All care and sorrow cease;
Remember 'tis His will
  Who hath spoken, "Peace!"

Strength for to-day, in house and home,
  To practice forbearance sweetly;
To scatter kind words and loving deeds,
  Still trusting in God completely.

A volume of this kind, it is supposable, will be more or less frequently referred to in future years, to revive fading recollections and recall pleasant associations; and, therefore, though it is so easy to moralize, it seems eminently fitting that helpful suggestions should accompany familiar autographs.

Let me say, then, that while in your youth a favorable combination of circumstances permits so much of happiness, the conditions of its enjoyment cannot always remain as now.

As the responsibilities, at present borne for you, shall come to rest on your own shoulders, and the darker shades of life's history are unfolded, you will find the peace, which floweth like a river, only in the degree in which you resolutely perform every known duty; and, forgetting your own wants— whether fancied or real—devote your thoughts, as well as your energies, to making the society in which you move happier for your being.

That you may indulge in no selfish ease; but bestow, as well as enjoy, a full share of the pleasures of time, and afterward receive a crown of glory, is the earnest wish of your friend—

The brave man is not he who feels no fear, for that were brutish and irrational; but he whose noble soul its fears subdues, and bravely dares the danger nature shrinks from.

Keep thy spirit pure from worldly taint
By the repellent strength of virtue;
Think on noble thoughts and deeds
    ever;
Count o'er the rosary of truth;
And practice precepts which are proven
    wise
It matters not then what thou fearest—
Walk boldly and wisely in the light
    thou hast;
There is a hand above will help thee on.

From the rising of the sun unto the going down of the same, my name shall be writ among your dearest friends.

Every man stamps his value on himself. The price we challenge for ourselves is given us. Man is made great or little by his own will.

Possessions vanish,
And opinions change,
And passion holds a fluctuating seat ;
But, subject neither to eclipse nor wane,
Duty remains.

    Happy be thy lot in life,
      Troubles scarcely known,
    Much of joy, but little strife,
      And plenty all thine own.

The older the ruin, the greener the moss.
The older the friendship, the keener the loss.

That one who can work right on, quietly waiting for recognition, if it come: if not, yet right on, is the true nobleman.

Dost thou know, love, that thy smile
  Makes the whole world bright for me
Just as sunrise pours a sudden
  Purple glory on the sea.
Ah! had I that power, ever
  Should the world look bright to thee.

I know not what to write about,
  So many themes are pressing;
All good enough in very truth,
  But quite unprepossessing:
Each moment of thy future life,
Live holy, whether maid or wife.

And let it be thy constant care,
  Midst earthly joy and sorrow,
By watchfulness and fervent prayer,
  Each this day and to-morrow,
To be prepared when Christ shall come,
His heaven to make thy final home.

Diamond little dewdrops, glistening
  in the sun,
We dwell upon your beauty even
  when you're gone;
Pure, unselfish motives, deeds of kindness done,
Shine as bright as dewdrops glistening
  in the sun.

Woman is especially honored of God. The world of affections is her world, not that of man's ambition; in that stillness which most becomes a woman, calm and holy, she sitteth by the fireside of the heart feeding its flames.

Oh, those eyes! so calm, serene—
Sweetest eyes were ever seen.
Will the woes of coming years
Ever shadow them with tears?
Shall my life the sunshine own,
That last night upon me shone,
When, beneath the summer skies,
Beamed on me those brown, brown eyes?

Speed slowly and gently, oh Time, in thy flight,
Let thy bounties be great and thy afflictions light.
Deal out full measure from thy store of wealth,
Give peace and plenty, success and good health.

Do your best, your very best,
   And do it every day;
Little boys and little girls
   That is the wisest way.

As you travel over life's rough highway, with liberal hand may you scatter seeds of kindness as you go, that when the great reaping time comes, your harvest may be abundant and blessed.

The bud, the flower, the fruit—how beautiful each in their own time. The change from one to the other so quiet and perfect, the last the fruition of the first.

God give you many days, and may your whole life be spotless and pure, giving beauty through all the changes, even when the leaf has turned brown and the fruit has ripened.

If we could see ourselves as others see us, how often we would have taken the other road.

Loveliness needs not the aid of foreign adornment.

Do all the good you can,
To all the people you can,
In all the ways you can,
Just as long as you can.

To persevere in one's duty and be silent, is the best answer to calumny.

Get but the truth once uttered, and 'tis like
 A star new-born, that drops into its place,
And which, once circling in its placid sound,
 Not all the tumult of the earth can shake.

Thanks to the human heart by which we live,
 Thanks to its tenderness, its joys and fears;
To me the meanest flower that blows can give
 Thoughts that do often lie too deep for tears.

True friends are like diamonds,
 Precious but rare.
False ones like Autumn leaves,
 Found everywhere.

Remember there is no spot in the universe to which you can retreat from your influence upon others.

Love thyself last; cherish those hearts
　　that hate thee;
Corruption wins not more than honesty.
Still in thy right hand carry gentle
　　peace,
To silence envious tongues. Be just,
　　and fear not.
Let all the ends thou aim'st at be thy
　　country's,
　　　Thy God's, and truth's.

Worlds may pass away and perish,
　　Every feeling die away,
But the constant love I cherish,
　　Never shall decay.

　　No.　Rest is not quitting
　　　　This busy career;
　　Rest is the fitting
　　　　Of self to its sphere.

　　It is the brook's motive
　　　　All clear without strife;
　　'Tis fleeting to ocean,
　　　　Beyond this brief life.

　　'Tis loving and serving
　　　　The highest and best;
　　'Tis onward, unswerving,
　　　　And this is true rest.

Long on thy cheeks may roses bloom,
   And all the charms which health bespeak;
But longer still thy gentle breast,
   Be ever Virtue's lovely seat.

I write these simple lines for thee,
Whene'er you see them think of me.

There is a plant that never dies,
   'Tis not of earth, but Heaven;
'Tis tinged with pure celestial dyes,
Its odors wafted to the skies
   By breeze a tempest driven.
'Tis not a tender fragile thing,
   It strengthens in the storm,
And midst the dreary waste
   It stands, a soul inspiring form.
     'Tis *thine, Friendship, thine.*

No rubies on the Indian shore
   Outshine thy *noble* mind;
Its radiance far exceeds them all,
   And *blesses* human kind.

A heart of *heavenly* purity
   Is laid within thy breast;
And ever for the weary soul,
   It breathes some tone of *rest.*

May it be your pleasure to cultivate those virtues which so gracefully adorn the character of a true woman and serves as a beacon light to those who are beneath and weaker than you.

Life is the bright dream of youth and the reality of age.

If we only do all the good we can,
  Though our ways lie far asunder,
If our souls grow purer and our lives more grand,
  We shall surely meet up yonder.

I most sincerely wish that you
May have many friends, and who,
No matter what you are passing through,
Will stick as close as good strong glue.

Life's a jest and all things show it,
I thought so once, and now I know it.

He who complies against his will
Is of his own opinion still.

On the battlefield of life
May you more than victor be.

While God's blessings are being showered so freely upon humanity
May a goodly portion fall on thee.

On the last leaf I write my name,
And though the last, still may it claim
　The tribute of a thought.
After more worthy friends receive
The attention you to each would give,
　I pray forget *me not*.

　The spirit which you possess is from above—pure, gentle, and kind. May it always be watered from above and refreshed by the gentle streams which flow from that fountain proceeding from the throne of God.
　And as the waters, rivers and streamlets run into the ocean, and centre there, to swell the unfathomable depths, so may the fruits of thy spirit run, and centre in God.
　Be careful of it for it will sweeten life's bitterest cup.

　As you travel through life, scatter kind words and gentle deeds; in so doing, you will enrich your soul. Withhold them, and it tends to poverty.

These little souvenirs possess not their greatest value when first written; but as time, with scythe in hand, passes along, and we are left standing, we are not the same, but these lines remain. Some, to cheer the saddened by awakening slumbering memories of better things; and others serving as guideboards on the road to eternity.

May your life be like the day—more beautiful in the evening; like the summer—aglow with promise; and, like the autumn, rich with the golden sheaves, where good works and deeds have ripened on the field.

Let the road be rough and dreary,
    And its end far out of sight;
Foot it bravely—strong or weary;—
    Trust in God, and do the right.

Life is but a day at best,
Sprung from night—in darkness lost;
Hope not sunshine every hour;
Fear not—clouds will always lower.

Know how sublime a thing it is
    To suffer and be strong.

Will one wandering thought of thine
   Rest its rapid flight on me?
Or to forgetfulness consign
   The friend that loves to think of thee.
Ah! sure thy fancy oft will dwell
   On scenes which once were dear to thee,
And when these lines you chance to read,
   You smiling will remember me.

Press on! our life is not a dream—
Though often such its mazes seem.
We were not born to live at ease—
Ourselves alone to aid and please.
To each a daily task is given:
A labor that shall fit for heaven,
When duty calls—let love grow warm,
Amid the sunshine or the storm,
With faith—life's trials boldly breast,
Then come a conqueror to thy rest.

   Meanness shun, and all its train;
   Goodness seek, and life is gain.

     If I wake, or if I sleep,
     Still the memory I keep
     Of the tender light that lies
     In the depths of those brown eyes.

Be blessings scattered o'er thy way,
  My gladsome, joyous, laughing sprite;
Be thy whole life one summer's day
  Without the night.

Trust not the world: It hath a smile
  And sunny garniture of bloom,
Which charms the eye a little while,
  And bids the soul forget the tomb;
The pomp and pageantry it wears
  To lure the spirit from its God,
Are crossed by doubt and dimmed by care
  And scourged by stern affliction's rod.

Oft as thine eye shall fondly trace
  These simple lines I sketch for thee,
Whate'er the time, where'er the place,
  O think of me.

When pleasure sparkles in thine eye,
  And every scene is fair to see,
When swift away the moments fly,
  O then remember me.

Whate'er may be my future lot in life---or dark or bright---sweet thoughts of *thee* will come as welcome guests with each revolving hour; and as I trace on memory's tablet the impression fair of thine untiring care, thy watchful love, thy kind forbearance to another's faults, my heart will yearn for thee, and for the tried affection.

If ever love's fondest prayer brought blessings from on high, thou shaīt be blessed. Friend! farewell! To him on whom thy cheerful hope relies, whose arm sustains thee, and whose promise soothes—my faith commends thee—may'st thou still receive grace for grace, and love for love; and guidance through this wilderness of tears! till thou possess thy Crown of Life.

On this leaf, in memory prest,
May my name forever rest.

On this page I'll write,
Simply to indite
My name as your friend.

But well thou play'd'st the housewife's part,
And all thy threads with magic art
Have wound themselves about this heart.

Cling to those who cling to you,
In the end there'd be but precious few
When they are tried and true;
So cling to those who cling to you.

Dear girl, I will write in thy book one line,
'Tis only to show you my friendship is thine;
As long as my heart in my bosom shall beat,
The throb of pure friendship for thee 'twill repeat.

Farewell; how oft that sound of sadness,
  Like thorns of sorrow pierce the heart,
And hush the harp tones of its gladness,
  And tear the bleeding chords apart.

Farewell! and if by distance parted
  We see each other's face no more,
Ah! may we with the faithful-hearted
  Meet beyond this parting shore.

Hours are golden links, God's token,
  Reaching heaven but one by one,
Take them lest the charm be broken
  Ere the pilgrimage be done.

Be content with thy lot,
  Though it may be small,
Each must have their share,
  One cannot have it all.

Industry is fortune's right hand,
And frugality its companion.

And thou, too, whosoe'er thou art,
  That readest this brief psalm,
As one by one thy hopes depart,
  Be resolute and calm.

May your coffee and slanders against you be ever the same—without grounds.

May thy life happy be,
Is my dear wish for thee.

It never pays to fret and growl
  When fortune seems our foe,
The better bred will push ahead
  And strike the braver blow;
    For luck is work,
    And those who shirk
  Should not lament their doom,
    But yield the play,
    And clear the way,
  That better men have room.

All the paths of faith, tho' severed wide,
O'er which the feet of prayerful reverence pass,
Meet at the gate of Paradise at last.

Desire not to live long, but well;
How long we live, not years, but actions, tell.

A beautiful life ends not in death.
Friendship above all ties doth bind the heart,
And faith in friendship is the noblest part.

There is a bright and precious gem,
　Lovely to behold;
'Tis seldom seen, and mostly when
　We feel we are growing old.

Contentment is that little gem,
　And if you have it not,
Take and cherish it, and then
　Happy be thy lot.

As hope is the anchor of the soul, so he is wise that is honest.

Scorn to do a mean action.

The sweetest pleasures are the soonest gone. Do nothing without design.

Age and youth both have their dreams, Youth looks at the possible, age at the probable.

You will profit much by learning the luxury of doing good.

As perfume is to the rose, so is good nature to the lovely.

Oh, never can we know how dear
  Each loved one is, till we have known
The deep regret, the bitter tear,
  That comes when those loved ones
    are gone.

Useful and steady may thy life proceed,
  Mild every word,
Good-natured every deed.
  Never with one thou lovest contend,
    But bear a thousand frailties
  From your friend.

Remember me is all I ask,
And, if remembrance be a task,
    Forget me.

Farewell! perhaps forever,
Beloved one adieu!
Wilt thou this token please to take,
And keep it long for friendship's sake;
And when these lines you chance to see,
Remember, that they came from me.

Round went the autograph; hither it came,
For me to write in; so here's my name.

Old friends and true friends!
Don't talk to me of new friends;
   The old are the best,
   Who stand the test,
Who book their name as *through* friends.

We meet and part—the world is wide;
We journey onward side by side
A little while, and then again
Our paths diverge. A little pain—
A silent yearning of the heart
For what has grown of life a part;
A shadow passing o'er the sun,
Then gone, and light again has come.
We meet and part, and then forget;
And life holds blessings for us yet.

When things don't go to suit you,
　　And the world seems upside down,
Don't waste your time in fretting,
　　But drive away the frown.

Passing through life's field of action,
　　Lest we part before its end,
Take within your modest volume,
　　This memento from a friend.

It never pays to wreck the health
　　In drudging after gain;
And he is sold who thinks that gold
　　The cheapest bought with pain
　　　　An humble lot,
　　　　A cosey cot,
　　Have tempted even kings;
　　　　For station high,
　　　　That wealth will buy,
　　Not oft contentment brings.

The world is full of fools,
　　And he who would none view,
Must shut himself in a cave,
　　And break his mirror, too.

Friendship, thou gift of heavenly birth
Misused, nay more—profaned—on
　　　earth,

Methinks long years have flown,
  And, sitting in her old arm-chair,
  ——— has older grown.
With silver sprinkled in her hair,
Her album thus she holds,
  And turns its many pages o'er,
And wonders if it still contains
  The memories of yore.
As o'er these pages thus she runs,
  With many a sigh and kiss,
Then suddenly she stops and says,
  "Who could have written this?"

———, life is all before you,
  Stretched out in its misty sheen,
And the future, though now hidden,
  Holds much joy for thee, I ween,
Why, then, seek to know what's coming,
  It is forming day by day,
But your heart, in blind out-reaching,
  Makes to-morrow of to-day.

"Life is real—life is earnest;
  And the heroine in the strife
Is the one who leaves the future—
  Living but the present life—
Lives it truly, nobly, grandly,
  Thus prepares for coming fate,
Strives to make her living perfect;—
  Learns to labor and to wait.

The violet is for faithfulness,
    Which in me shall abide;
Hoping, likewise, from your heart,
    You will not let it slide.

This is thine album. May it be
A source of happiness to thee.
And may each page that's written o'er,
Be better than the one before.

Perform your duties without fear,
    Will make your pathway bright and
        clear;
Falter, stop, and leave undone,
    Will make it like the clouded sun.

Some folks are constantly wishing,
    I could never get much for a wish,
But should you ever go a fishing,
    May your net be will filled with fish.

    Happiness: a phantom all are seeking, few can find.

On this page of your album I scribble,
    Now, remember, no critic must see,
But once in awhile peep at it yourself,
    Then remember 'twas scribbled by
        me.

May you always have a full share,
  With a surplus on the shelf,
And ever be ready to share
  With those who have less than yourself.

In this world of change and sorrow, when shall we meet again?

May you always have enough and plenty for each day,
May you never have enough to waste or throw away,
May you live long enough your debts to pay,
May you never live so long as to be in other people's way.

If I should make a wish for you it would be this: I wish you a large share of success in your pursuit of happiness; may your efforts in the direction of right bring abundant reward. I would not wish your pathway to be over flowers only; God made the rose and thorn to go together; let us not separate them, but with you may the roses be many and the thorns few.

The little bee so silently
　　Gathers honey from the flower,
So may you as quietly
　　Find pleasure in each hour.

May your life be as bright as the stars
　　of the night,
And of the sun whose light always
　　dazzles the sight;
May you never lose sight, sure as black
　　is not white,
Of the fact that the right will always
　　make might.

　　Twilight lets the curtain down,
　　And pins it with a star.

'Tis beauty that doth make woman
　　proud,
'Tis virtue that doth make her most
　　admired,
'Tis modesty that makes her seem
　　divine.

As sunshine and rain, pleasure and
　　pain,
　　Each day on some must fall,
So the wise thing to do, if we only knew,
　　Is to make the best of it all.

One long sweet spring be thine
With buds still bursting forth,
Fresh blossoms every hour,
And verdure fair and new.
Peace be thy gentle guest,
Peace, holy and divine,
God's blessed sunlight still
Upon thy pathway shine.

How gay and how happy, how charming and fair
Are these sweet little songsters that fly through the air;
With sweet rolling carols they glide in their glee,
Whatever their lot, they are happy and free.
May your life be as theirs, ever happy and bright,
With a heart and a face to shed sunshine and light;
When with one you shall meet—fondest joy of your life,
You should love him and make him a happy, good wife.

Whoever thinks a faultless piece to see,
Thinks what ne'er was, nor is, nor ne'er can be.

Shall I tell you of an evening
  When the snow lay on the ground,
When the wintry wind was silent,
  And the sky with stars was crowned?
When the parlor looked so pleasant,
  And the world to me so bright,
As we sat together dreaming
  In the flick'ring firelight?

Nay, I will not, for it may be
  That your own heart longeth sore
For the olden time caresses
  From the one who comes no more;
For, perhaps, you have your sorrow
  Buried deep within your breast;
And, perhaps, you have *your* moments
  When your spirit cries for rest.

'Tis sweet to be remembered.

In the course of our reading we should lay up in our minds a store of goodly thoughts in well-wrought words, which shall be a living treasure of knowledge always with us, and from which, at various times, and amidst all the shifting circumstances, we might be sure of drawing some comfort, guidance and sympathy.

Joy's opening buds, affection's glowing
   flowers,
  Once lightly sprang within thy beam-
   ing track.
O! life was beautiful in those lost
   hours!
  And yet you cannot wish to wander
   back;
Nay! thou may'st love in loneliness to
   think
  On pleasures past, though never more
   to be;
Hope links thee to the future, but the
   link
  That binds thee to the past is memory.

Sweet is the hour that brings us home,
  Where all will spring to meet us,
Whose hands are striving as we come
  To be the first to greet us.

When the world has spent its frowns
   And wrath,
  And cares are sorely pressing,
'Tis sweet to turn from our roving path,
  And find a fireside blessing.

   Keep to the right as you are passing
along, giving your neighbor full half
of the road.

Bright sunny hope, thy radiant beam
Smiles sweetly on life's troubled dream.

———

May humble hope your portion be,
'Till launched into eternity.

———

Like the unsullied little dew-drop,
   Shining brightly in the sun,
With heaven's brightest colors,
   Softly blending into one,
A pure and spotless woman
   Man's love has always won;
The blending of her virtues
   Is a diamond in the sun.

———

Dear ———, at thy wish I write,
And in this book some thought indite,
I scarce know what—a wish sincere
Some lonely moment of thine to cheer,
May every lasting joy be thine,
Refulgent virtue round thee shine.
Wilt thou revere the winding road
Which leads beyond to a bright abode,
That when thy journeys here are o'er,
Will meet again on the eternal shore.

———

Worthy to love, fondly to devote ourselves to the happiness of another who deserves our highest regard, is not condemned by religion; it is not even a weakness which it permits or deplores, but a virtue which it sanctions and commends.

The heart that is deceived or betrayed need not augment its anguish by self-reproach.

Love is not an innocent but a noble passion. When guided by principle it is the gem of all social virtues—the cement and solace of the virtuous relations of the human life.

When rewarded with the hallowed possession of its object, it strews the path of duty with flowers, but when unfortunate and ill-requited, it becomes so absorbed in high and holy principles, investing resignation with unwonted sublimity, and extracting from earthly disappointment the calmer satisfaction of heavenly hope. The process by which it is thus transformed may impair the frail tenement which enshrines it; and the dross of mortality, in such a furnace, may melt away into its kindred earth. But the unrobed spirit returns to God who gave it, and at last enjoys repose where it first derived existence.

That every kindly wish and thought,
  By friends expressed within these
    pages,
Be yours, and trials common to us all,
  May cross your path by "easy stages."

Remember me when far away,
  And only half awake;
Remember me on your wedding day,
  And send a slice of cake.

When worth and beauty prompt the
  line,
Perhaps a pen as poor as mine
    May be forgiven
To try and write of things divine,
    And think of heaven!
But pause, rash verse! and don't abuse
A bashful maiden's ear with news
    Of her own beauty!
And yet no other theme I'll choose,
    Or think a duty!
So, then, for fear I might offend,
I'll say, *God bless her!*—and thus end.

—— is your name,
  Single is your station,
Happy be the little man
  That makes the alteration.

ALBUM VERSES.

The earth can boast no purer tie,
  No brighter, richer gem,
No jewel of a lovelier dye,
  Than Friendship's diadem.

Then may this ray of light divine,
  Ne'er from our bosoms fade;
But may it on our pathway shine,
  Till death our hearts invade.

'Tis a terrible fate, my dear miss,
To be asked to write in a book like this;
For, scratch my head as hard as I may—
    I've such a skull—
And if I try to moralize,
  Or vent my thoughts in sentiment,
Or attempt to laud you to the skies,
  Or spread myself on compliment,
    I'm so awful dull,
That my efforts would prove futility;
  For the sex of your kind, are of that
    turn of mind,
That morals, verse and flattery,
  Have to you been so oft defined,
    You are full,
If rhyming I try, adorable Miss,
  The first I think of, is dear little Kiss,
Or some such nonsense as connubial
  bliss,

Or changing your title "Mrs." from
    "Miss;"
        But that's prosaical.
To give you advice I'd never pre-
    sume;—
    Incompetence may be the reason for
        that;—
To wish you long life and a blest happy
    home
    Is aged and stale, exhausted and flat,
        And excruciatingly formal.
Now, what to do I do not know,
    Or how to make my paragraph;
So I'll doff my hat, and make my bow
    And send this as my autograph.

———

May there be just clouds enough o'er your life to cause a glorious sunset.

———

Thy cheerful, gentle ways, I do admire;
Thy future to be happy I greatly
    desire;
Thy trusting confidence, may I require;
Thy firm friend to be, will I aspire.

———

In memory's wreath may one bud be entwined for me.

Oh! love is such a strange affair;
So strange to all.
    It cometh from above
    And lighteth like a dove
                On some.
    But some it never hits
    Unless it gives them fits.
                Oh, hum.

As a slight token of esteem,
    Accept these lines from me;
So plain and simple, they do seem
    Unworthy such as thee.
But soon these traced lines will fade
    And disappear—'tis their doom.
May you, unlike them, be arrayed
    In a perpetual bloom.

MISCELLANEOUS.

In times of prosperity our friends are many,
But the time of adversity tries and proves them.

Gems of price are deeply hidden,
  'Neath the rugged rocks concealed;
What would ne'er come forth unbidden,
  To thy search may be revealed.

If recollections of friends brighten moments of sadness,
  What a fund of delight is here treasured for thee!
If advice and kind wishes bring goodness and gladness,
  How perfect and happy thy future must be.

May e'en thy failings lean to virtue's side.

ALBUM VERSES.

While the fading flowers of pleasure,
  Spring spontaneous from the soil;
Thou wilt find the harvest's treasure
  Yields alone to patient toil.

The tissues of the Life to be—
  We weave with colors all our own,
And in the field of Destiny,
  We reap as we have sown.

There is seldom a line of glory written upon earth's face, but a line of suffering runs parallel with it; and they that read the lustrous syllables of the one, and stoop not to decipher the spotted and worn inscription of the other, get the least half of the lesson that earth has to give.

How beautiful your book, from end to end,
And every page a room to lodge a friend;
Fain would I enter with a seemly grace,
Attired and mannered as befits the place;
But best endeavor falls below the aim
And rests at last, content to leave a name.

Hours are golden links—God's token—
Reaching heaven but one by one;
Take them, lest the chain be broken
Ere thy pilgrimage be done.

The brave man is not he who feels no fear,
For that were stupid and irrational;
But he whose noble soul its fears subdues,
And bravely dares the danger nature shrinks from.

Fling wide the portals of your heart!
Make it a temple set apart
From earthly use, for Heaven's employ—
Adorned with prayer and love and joy;
So shall your Sovereign enter in
And new and noble life begin.

We could count time by heart-throbs; he most lives who thinks most, speaks the noblest, acts the best.

We ourselves shape the joys and fears
Of which the life to come is made,
And fill our future atmosphere
With sunshine or with shade.

When the name that I write here is
 dim on the page,
And the leaves of your album are yellow
 with age,
Still think of me kindly, and do not
 forget
That, wherever I am, I remember you
 yet.

The massive gates of circumstance
 Are turned upon the slightest hinge,
And thus some seeming pettiest chance,
 Oft gives the life its after tinge.

Oh, for a home in Zululand, or Arctic
 regions cold,
A peasant's cot or hermit's hut, midst
 solitude untold,
With Kaffirs or with Hottentots, in
 Egypt or Leone—
'Twere bliss to live in *any* spot where
 albums are unknown.

In the golden chain of friendship regard me as a link.

Some write for pleasure, some write
 for fame,
But I write simply to sign my name.

Meanness shun and all its train;
Goodness seek and life is gain.

Strive to keep the "Golden Rule,"
And learn your lessons well at school.

Those that want friends must show themselves friendly.

If you have found the "pearl of great price," all the bliss of heaven will be yours.

Remember me when "far, far off,
Where the woodchucks die of whooping cough."

He is a coward who will not turn back,
When first he discovers he's on the wrong track.

May that love which has always existed grow stronger.

A little body often harbors a great soul.

Yours sincerely, in the bonds of friendship.

Apply thine heart unto knowledge.

What you do, do with your might.

Think much, speak little, write with care.

Not to go back is somewhat to advance.

Be good, do good, and you will be happy.

A smooth sea never made a skillful mariner.

Drop one pearl in memory's casket for your friend.

A good name is rather to be chosen than great riches.

Bow down thine ear, and hear the words of the wise.

That ye might walk worthy of the Lord unto all pleasing, being beautiful in every good work, and increasing in the knowledge of God, is the wish of your friend.

There are three lessons I would write,
　　Three words as with a burning pen
In tracings of eternal light
　　Upon the hearts of friends.

Have Hope. Though clouds environ now
　　And gladness hides her face in scorn,
Put thou the shadow from thy brow;
　　No night but hath its morn.

Have Faith. Where'er thy bark is driven,
　　The calm's disport, the tempest's mirth—
Know this. God rules the hosts of heaven,
　　The inhabitants of earth.

Have Love; and not alone for one,
　　But man as man thy brother call,
And scatter like the circling sun,
　　Thy charities on all.

Thus grave these lessons on thy soul:
　　Hope, Faith and Love; and thou shalt find
Strength when life's surges cease to roll,
　　Light where thou else wert blind.

Let your life be like a snowflake, which leaves a mark, but not a stain.

Within this book so pure and white,
Let none but friends presume to write;
And may each line with friendship given,
Direct the reader's thoughts to heaven.

   Leaf green on ground of white,
   My name, I fain would write
   That you remember still
   In June or in December chill,
     We two are friends.

Oh, wayward mortal who these books
    invented,
Why wast thou not by some kind hand
    prevented?
And thereby kept from many a luckless
    swain,
The direful knowledge that he lacked
    a brain—
Lacked it, at least, where poetry was
    needed,
Like the poor wight who here has not
    succeeded.

The large are not the sweetest flowers;
The long are not the happiest hours;
Much talk doth not much friendship
    tell;
Few words are best—I wish you well.

Through days of doubt and darkness,
   In fear and trembling breath,
Through mists of sin and sorrow,
   In tears and grief and death;

Through days of light and gladness,
   Through days of love and life,
Through smiles and joy and sunshine,
   Through days with beauty rife;

The Lord of life and glory,
   The king of earth and sea,
The Lord who guarded Israel;
   Keep watch, sweet friend, o'er thee.

Truth—Freedom—Virtue—these have
   power;
If rightly cherished, to uphold, sustain,
And bless thy spirit, in its darkest hour.

Thy own trim, modest form,
   Is always neatly clad,
Thou surely will make the tidiest wife
   That ever husband had.

Among the many friends who claim
   A kind remembrance in thy heart,
I too, would add my simple name,
     Among the rest.

To knit and spin was once a girl's employment;
But now to dress and have a beau is all the girl's enjoyment.

To fear no ill, to do no wrong to all men, to prove true—
This is the "golden rule" of life; let it be so to you.

Is it vain in life's wide sea,
To ask you to remember me?
Undoubtedly it is my lot,
Just to be known and then—forgot.

O no! The heart, which is the seat
  Of love like mine, can never rove;
Its faithful pulse may cease to beat,
  But never—never cease to love:
For love is past the earth's control
  And soaring as an ocean wave
It is eternal as the soul,
  And lives and blooms beyond the the grave.
It is a link of pleasure's chain,
  A never-ending token,
Whose lustre and whose strength remain,
  When all save that are broken.

May God's mercy ever guide thee,
　　Safe o'er all thy thorny road;
And His grace whate'er betide thee,
Lead thee home to His abode.

———

Begirt with roses of the royal June,
A resurrected day swings highest morn
In every year; and so through life I
　　pray
May never failing changes, bring their
　　day,
And flames of love in swinging censers
　　rise
While all thy thoughts leads on toward
　　the skies.

———

————, I'll write a line or two
　　On this fair page for thee,
And though I can't the rest outdo
　　Yet, this must do for me.

———

I cannot wish thee greater joys,
　　Than others here expressed,
But I respond with every power
　　To wish thee ever blessed.

———

　　In time we transact business for eternity; whatever, therefore, we do now, should be done well.

I'll pull a bunch of buds and flowers,
  And tie a ribbon round them,
If you'll but think in your lonely hours
  Of the little friend who bound them.
So here's your bunch of buds and flowers—
  And here's the ribbon round them,
And here to cheer your sadder hours
Is the little friend who bound them.

"Forget me not" when far away
Amidst a thoughtless world you stray
"Forget me not" when fools would win
Your footsteps to the paths of sin.
"Forget me not" when urged to wrong
By fashions and temptations strong.
"Forget me not" when pleasure's snare
Would keep you from the house of prayer.
"Forget me not" in feeble age,
E'en let me then your thoughts engage.
"Forget me not" when death shall close
These eyelids in their last repose,
And murm'ring breezes softly wave
Perchance the grass upon my grave.
Whate'er thy age and lot may be,
Long as thy life shall last remember me.

Friend! Trust* not, cling not, to the hope
  Of constancy below.
Earth's fragile blossoms smile and drop,
  Her waters ebb and flow.

Yet time to time some joys may blight,
  Some finer feelings chill,
But may'st thou hold one hope of light
  Unchanged, unclouded still.

The hope to win in realms above
  Of bright and boundless range,
A world of constancy and love,
  A world that cannot change.

Small service is true service while it lasts;
  Of friends, however humble, scorn not one:
The daisy, by the shadow that it casts,
  Protects the lingering dew-drop from the sun.

Every hour comes to us charged with duty, and the moment it is past returns to Heaven to register itself how spent.

There is a Divinity that shapes our ends,
Rough-hew them how we will.

Make good use of time if thou lovest eternity; yesterday cannot be recalled; to-morrow cannot be secured; to-day only is thine, which, if once lost, is lost forever.

May each thought be pure and sincere,
  Addressed upon these spotless pages;
Reflections fond, they'll always prove,
Youthful friend, through many ages.

They who have light in themselves, will not revolve as satellites.

Through time we'll change, and then,
  This little book will somewhat bind us;
You'll take it up, and think of me,
  And all the joys we've left behind us.

As the shadow of the sun is the largest when his beams are lowest, so we are always least when we make ourselves the greatest.

Our eyes see all around in gloom or glow,
Hues of their own, fresh borrowed from the heart.

Across the page of spotless white
Friends trail the pen, and in our sight
Grow precious all the lines they write.

As for some white-sailed ship at sea,
So, little book, my watch for thee;
Return with freight of love to me.

Why, of course, I will write
Just what my thoughts may indite,
  In this, your leaves of affection;
And I hope your life without one flaw,
May secure a real nice mother-in-law,
  So that you may feel no dejection.

Let Fate do her worst; there are
    relics of joy,
Bright dreams of the past, she cannot
    destroy;
They come in the night-time of sorrow
    and care,
And bring back the features that joy
    used to wear.
Like the vase, in which roses have once
    been distilled,
You may break—you may shatter—the
    vase, if you will;
But the scent of the roses will hang
    round it still.

If you wish success in life make perseverance your bosom friend, experience your wise counsel, caution your elder brother, and hope your guardian genius.

Count that day lost whose low descending sun
    Views from thy hand no worthy action done.

'Tis but a trifle that you ask,
  But this you will admit,
That trifles, more than greater tasks,
  Will sometimes strain our wit.
I wish thee health, and wealth, and joy,
  As others have before:
And were I in poetic mood,
  I'd surely wish thee more.

May you still be given
Strength for each day in house and home
  To practice forbearance sweetly,
To scatter kind words and loving deeds,
  Trusting in God completely.

Your character cannot be essentially injured except by your own acts.

Write your name by kindness, love and mercy, upon the hearts of those you come in contact with, and you will never be forgotten.

Recollect that trifles make perfection, and that perfection is no trifle.

Here's a sigh for those who love me,
    And a smile for those who hate,
And whatever sky's above me,
    Here's a heart for every fate.

In all thy humors, whether grave or mellow,
Thou art such a touchy, testy, pleasant fellow;
Hast so much wit, and mirth, and spleen, about thee,
There is no living with thee nor without thee.

I write here a name which I hope shall be known
To all of the ages which follow my own.
"How conceited!" you say; but my lines shall remain;
'Tis my hope, you'll discover, not I, that is vain.

Our greatest glory consists not in never falling, but in rising every time we fall.

Though many miles apart
   Our homes may prove to be,
Yet in the recess of your heart
   Keep one kind thought of me.

Always have a willing hand
Full of kind deeds,
For many needs;
Also have a loving heart most.

Great truths are portions of the soul of
   man ;
   Great souls are portions of eternity;
Each drop of blood that e'er through
   true heart ran
   With lofty message, ran for thee and
      me;
For God's law, since the starry song
   began,
   Hath been, and still forevermore
      must be,
That every deed which shall outlast
   Time's span
   Must goad the soul to be erect and
      free.

True friends, like ivy and the wall,
Both stand together or together fall.

Hearts, like doors, can ope' with ease,
To very, very little keys;
And don't forget that they are these:
"I thank you sir," and "if you please."

May you live in bliss, from sorrow away,
Having plenty laid up for a rainy day;
And when you are ready to settle in life,
May you find a good husband and make a good wife.

Our lives are albums; each new day's a page
  As spotless as the leaf on which I write.
Whene'er those books of ours shall be read,
  May few unwise inscriptions meet the sight.

On the broad highway of action
Friends of worth are far and few;
But when one has proved her friendship,
Cling to her who clings to you.

Blessings real and a brighter hope for time and eternity.

Were mine the power, I'd twine for thee
  A crown of jewels rare;
Each gem should be a kingdom,
  Each pearl an humble prayer.

There are few friends in this wide world
Whose love is fond and true;
But, ———, when you count them o'er
Place me among the few.

With a heart free from care, and my
    home in the West,
  I'll pace the broad deck with a light
    throbbing breast,
Yet still as I dream of those days that
    are gone,
  Of the gay happy hours in my own
    native home,
Far, far o'er the wave my heart wanders
    there
  To its shrine of devotion, where youth,
    free from care,
We spent such golden hours of inno-
    cence and glee
  With you and dear companions, so
    pray remember me.

May you always be happy,
    And live at your ease;
Get a kind husband,
    And do as you please.

———

May thy heart beat with purest hopes
    To pity and to bless,
And strive to make earth's comforts more,
    Its pains and follies less.

———

Love's but a baby that passionate
    Cries to be mated at birth:
Time isn't lost if it teaches you
    What a good woman is worth.

———

There is a small and simple flower
    That twines around the humblest cot,
And in the sad and lonely hours
    It whispers low: "Forget me not."

———

When asked in an album to write,
    I feel quite inclined to refuse;
For what should I dare to indite
    That would a young lady amuse?
Not wit, for I have none of that,
    Nor romance—my fancy is tame;
And compliments sound so flat,
    I'm forced to write merely my name.

What if the waiting be wearisome,
  What if the work days be drear:
Time, the old thief, cannot rob you
  Of fifty-two Sundays a year.

There is many a rest on the road of life,
  If we only would stop to take it,
And many a tone from the better land,
  If the querulous heart would wake it.
To the sunny soul that, full of hope,
  And whose beautiful trust ne'er faileth,
The grass is green and the flowers are bright,
  Though the wintry storm prevaileth.

  Little minds are tamed and subdued by misfortune, but great minds rise above it.

Beauty is but a vain, a fleeting good,
  A shining gloss that fadeth suddenly,
A flower that dies when almost in the bud,
  A bright glass that breaketh suddenly;
A fleeting good, a glass, a gloss, a flower,
  Lost, faded, broken, dead within the hour.

May she for whom these lines are penned
By using well, make time her friend;
Then whether he stands still or flies,
Whether the moment lives or dies,
She need not care; for time will be
Her friend, to all eternity.

All the blessings of this life are nothing worth without the sunshine of hope for a bright and lasting future. My wishes are these for thee.

May happiness ever be thy lot,
  Wherever thou shalt be;
And joy and pleasure light the spot
  That may be home to thee.

How sweet to have a faithful friend,
  In whom we can confide:
To bless us if we act aright,
  And if we err to chide.

Hope the best, get ready for the worst, and take what God sends.

Be content with the lot God has marked out for you. Love, honor and obey Him in all things, and your last days will be peaceful and happy.

The cheek is pale with thought, but not
  from woe,
  And yet so lovely that if mirth could
  flush
  Its rose of whiteness with the brightest blush,
My heart would wish away the ruddier
  glow;
And dazzle not thy deep blue eyes—
  but oh!
  While gazing on them—sterner eyes
  will gush,
  And into mine my mother's weakness rush,
Soft as the last drops round heaven's
  airy bow;
For, through thy long dark lashes low
  depending,
  The soul of melancholy Gentleness
Gleams like a Seraph from the sky
  descending.
  Above all pain—yet pitying all
  distress,
At once such majesty with sweetness
  blending,
  I worship more but cannot love thee
  less.

May the morn of thy life be bright and joyous, the noontide peaceful and happy, and the sunset gloriously hopeful, is the wish of your friend.

———

Life, Death and Immortality—these three—the first, the Road—the second, the Gate. May you walk safely the first, pass triumphantly the second, and rest forever in the third.

———

Although I am advised not to write fast,
I hope the thought I would express may last.

———

Methinks that many years have flown
   And in a large arm-chair,
——— is sitting older grown
   With silver in her hair.

And thus she muses, as she wipes
   Her glasses o'er and o'er:
I wonder if my album keeps
   The memories of yore.

She turns the pages through and through
   With many a sigh and kiss,
When suddenly she stops and says,
   Who could have written this?

Three friends that never fail
  Each mortal hath,
Himself, his God, and last
  The Angel, Death.

Dearer than power or fame
  Or hoarded pelf,
Nearer than brother's love—
  The love of self.

Truer than sun or star,
  Higher than Heaven,
Deeper than neither space
  God's love is given.

More gentle than the Spring
  Or Summer's breath,
And as a Mother kind,
  The Angel—Death.

Yes, ———, I will write my name
  In here, as you request;
And, if to you it's all the same,
I'll add a line—though rather tame—
  For Critic's eyes, as my bequest.

My wishes and my hopes for you,
  Find glad expression here;
Although, indeed, it's very true,
There is no room for all that's due
  To one we hold so dear.

Good health—first wish of all—
   Of all God's gifts the best;
A happy heart that loves to call
On Him who notes the sparrow's fall
   And promises sweet rest.

Although beset by worldly care,
   Fix all your hopes on Heaven,
And view by faith the glories fair,
Which, in that world beyond the air,
   To faithful ones are given.

May the Angels twine for thee
A wreath of immortality.

The night has a thousand eyes—
    The day but one;
Yet the light of the whole world dies
    With the setting sun.

The mind has a thousand eyes—
    The day but one;
Yet the light of the whole world dies
    When love is done.

   It has been beautifully said: The water that flows from a spring does not congeal in winter; and those sentiments which flow from the heart cannot be chilled by adversity.

You ask for your Album a rhyme;
  With pleasure I hear and obey;
Refusal were folly or crime—
  For who could to ——— say "nay?"

   There's many a trouble
   Would break like a bubble,
And into the waters of Lethe depart,
   Did not we rehearse it
   And tenderly nurse it,
And give it a permanent place in the heart.
   Resolve to be merry,
   All worry to ferry,
Across the famed waters that bid us forget.
   And no longer fearful,
   But happy and cheerful,
We feel life has much that's worth living for yet.

May we always remain as good friends as we are neighbors.

On this spotless page my pen essays to trace a record of affection; and, as I write, a wish is in my heart that, for thee, every life-leaf will be written with the golden pen of love.

Beautiful faces are those that wear
The light of a pleasant spirit there,
It matters little if dark or fair.

———

Long may Heaven's protecting arm
  Shield thee, ———, from all harm.

———

Be kind to all; be intimate with few;
And may the few be well chosen.

———

Evils in the journey of life are like the hills which alarm travelers upon their road; they both appear great in the distance, but when we approach them, we find them far less insurmountable than we had conceived.

———

Miss ——— ! O Miss ——— !
What can I write that's new
Among so very many
Pretty compliments to you?
In poetry, I fear I'd fail—
I'm very sure I'd stammer—
You cannot drive the ponderous nail
With a small ten-cent tack hammer.
Since, then, so high I cannot soar,
Nor chirp notes like the lark,
Please cancel what I've said before,
I'll simply make my mark.

If a body ask a body,
 In her book to write;
If a body refuse a body,
 Need a body fight?

All the lassies and the laddies
 Write sweet things herein;
If a body write less sweetly,
 Does a body sin?

May Future, with her kindest smile,
 Wreath laurels for thy brow;
May loving angels guard and keep thee
 Ever pure as thou art now.

If writing in Albums remembrance insures,
With the greatest of pleasure I'll scribble in yours.

In after years when you recall
 The days of pleasures past,
And think of joyous hours and all
 Have flown away so fast,
When some forgotten air you hear
 Brings back past scenes to thee,
And gently claims your listening ear
 Keep one kind thought for me.

When years and months have glided by,
  And on this page you cast your eye,
Remember 'twas a friend sincere
That left this kind remembrance here.
With best wishes for your future cheer.

Dear ———, may your life be blest
With friendship, love and happiness;
May all your friends prove true,
And cheer you all the journey through.

  This life is not all sunshine,
    Nor is it yet all showers;
  But storms and calms alternate,
    As thorns among the flowers;
  And while we seek the roses,
    The thorns full oft we scan,
  Still let us, though they wound us,
    Be happy as we can.

  This life has heavy crosses,
    As well as joys to share,
  And griefs and disappointments,
    Which you and I must bear;
  And if we may not follow
    The path our hearts would plan,
  Let us make all around us,
    As happy as we can.

May the hinges of our Friendship never rust.

May your days in joy be passed
  With friends to bless and cheer,
And each year exceed the last
  In all that earth holds dear.

Though many friends have signed their
    names,
  And some have left their mark,
I see a place for me remains
  To add my small remark.
My wish for thee is: joy through life;
  And bliss supreme, when some one's
    wife.

I pray the prayer of Plato old:
  God make thee beautiful within;
And let thine eye the good behold
  In everything save sin.

A few true friends to aid us and love
    us,
  And cordial hands to warmly clasp
    our own;
O! surely God hath never made us
  To live distrustingly, selfish, and
    alone.

A verse you ask this fine day:
  Of course I'll write you one.
The task of writing finds its pay
  In joy that it is done.

Why ask a name?
  Small is the good it brings;
Names are but breath—
  Deeds—deeds alone—are things.

The truest happiness is found in making others happy.

Accept my friend these lines from me,
They show that I remember thee,
And hope some thought they will retain
Till you and I shall meet again.

For thee, my fair and gentle friend,
I ask not wealth or fame,
I only ask thy path may be
Free from life's toil and care.

Among the many friends that claim
  A kind remembrance in thy breast,
I too would add my simple name,
  -Among the rest.

Never grow weary doing good.

May Heaven on you its choicest blessings shower
Is the sincere wish of your friend.

Let us try to be happy, we may if we will
Find some pleasure in life to o'erbalance the ill.
There was never an evil, if well understood,
But what, rightly managed, would turn to a good.

If we were but as ready to look to the light,
As we are to sit moping because it is night,
We would own it a truth, both in word and in deed
That who tries to be happy is sure to succeed.

Let us only in earnestness each do our best,
Before God and our conscience, and trust for the rest,
Still taking the truth, both in word and in deed,
That who tries to be happy is sure to succeed.

Keep me in remembrance,
If in the darkness
  I should stray afar,
    Like some lost traveler
With no guiding star.
Be then still my true,
  Sincere, and loving friend,
And o'er all ills and
  Trials to my life's end
    Keep me in remembrance.

I want a warm and faithful friend,
  To cheer the adverse hour;
Who ne'er to flatter will descend,
  Nor bend the knee to power;
A friend to chide me when I'm wrong;
  My inmost soul to see;
And that my friendship prove as strong
  For him as his for me.

Of all the gifts which heaven bestows
  There is one above all measure,
And that's a friend 'midst all our woes
  A friend, is found a treasure.

To thee I give this sacred name
  For thou are such to me,
And ever proudly will I claim
  To be a friend of thee,

ALBUM VERSES.

There is a flower, a lovely flower
   Tinged deep with faith's unchanging
      hue,
Pure as the ether, in its hour,
   Of loveliest and serenest blue;
The streamlet's gentle side it seeks,
   The quiet fount, the shaded grot,
And sweetly to the heart it speaks
   Forget me not! forget me not!

Then be not coy, but use your time,
   And while ye may, go marry;
For having lost but once your prime
   You may forever tarry.

   Be always kind-hearted,
      Do good deeds without end,
   But never forget,
      Your affectionate friend.

No night descend on thee,
   O'er thee no sorrows come;
Safe be thy journey through,
   Through this vale of cloud and gloom.

Hope's precious pearl in sorrow's cup
   Unmelted at the bottom lay,
To shine again, when all drank up;
   The bitterness should pass away.

Favor is deceitful and beauty is vain, but a woman that feareth the Lord she shall be praised.—Prov. xxxi, 30.

May the blessing of God be upon thee,
May the Sun of Glory shine 'round thy
    bed,
May the gates of plenty, honor and
    happiness be open to thee.
May no sorrow distress thy days,
May no griefs disturb thy nights;
May the pillow of peace kiss thy cheek,
And the pleasure of realization attend
    thy beautiful dreams.
And when length of days makes thee
Tired of earthly joys, and the curtain of
Death gently closes 'round thy last
    sleep of human existence,
May the Angel of God attend thy bed
    and
Take care that the expiring lamp of
    life
Shall not receive one rude blast to
    hasten on its extinction.

One by one thy griefs will meet thee,
  Do not fear an armed band;
One will fade as others greet thee,
  Shadows passing through the land.

If peace is to be your portion through life (and surely why not?) the Light of the World, which the scripture declares is Jesus, must ever be observed and obeyed. The hope of your friend is that "You may be kept in perfect peace by having your mind stayed on Christ Jesus."

I'm in a quandary how to compose
Doggerel rhymes and ditties for those
Albums so freely thrust under my nose.
Vain 'tis to strive 'gainst the Miss who decrees,
"An original poem, if you please,"
From your dull brain you must squeeze.
Fain would I fly—I care not where;
Lend me your wings, oh, angels fair,
Encounter another album I do not dare.
Can it be that there is no country bright,
Kept securely free from albums' blight?

So live, so act, that every hour,
May die as dies the natural flower,
A self-reviving thing of power,
That every word and every deed,
May bear within itself the seed
Of future good in future need.

With hope and faith for our beacon lights,
  While virtue guides our way,
Secure we'd pass temptations by,
  That would lead our hearts astray.
And each to the other kind and true
  While earth was our spirit's haven,
Would pray that we ne'er might part on earth
  But to meet again in heaven.

Help somebody worse off than yourself, and you will find you are better off than you fancied.

This book may fall asunder,
  Its pages dim with age;
The ink may lose its lustre
  Upon each shining page,
But she who writes these verses
  Shall ever, ever be,
Through all the world's reverses
  A faithful friend to thee.

Oh! for the power of Tennyson's pen!
  (By my failures to rhyme I'm dejected),
To tell all the world again and again,
  In your album how much I'm affected

May peace enfold thee in her downy
    wing,
  Pure songs around thee weave a fairy
    spell,
To heaven thy heart's deep longing
    cling,
  And happiness forever with thee
    dwell.

They say that love had once a book
  (The urchin likes to copy you),
Where all who came the pencil took,
  And wrote—like us—a line or two.

'Twas innocence, the maid divine,
  Who kept this volume bright and fair
And saw that no unhallowed line
  Or thought profane should enter
    there.

And daily did the pages fill
  With fond device and loving lore,
And every leaf she turned was still
  More bright than that she turned
    before.

  Heart is a hope-place, and home is a heart-place, and she is sadly mistaken who would exchange the happiness of home for anything less than heaven.

May angels weave for thee a crown of immortality.

Trust, my friend, no Siren's whisper,
    Weave no web in fancy's loom,
Build no castle for the future,
    For the golden days to come.
Life has more or less besetments,
    More or less of grief and woe,
Shadows always check our pathway,
    Sunbeams only come and go.
Cast thy bread upon the waters,
    Out upon the waves alone,
You will find it drifted to thee
    After many days have flown.
Ever hoping and enduring,
    Ever prayerful on the way,
May you reach the golden entrance
    Opening on eternal day.

I would not enter on my list
Of friends the man
Who needlessly sets foot upon a worm.
An inadvertant step may crush the snail
That crawls at evening in the public
    path;
But he that has humanity, forewarned,
Will tread aside and let the reptile live.

The bright black eye, the melting blue,
  I cannot choose between the two;
But that is dearest all the while
  Which means for us the sweetest smile.

I ask not a life for thee,
  All radiant as others have done,
But that life may have just enough shadow
  To temper the glare of the sun.

Thus as these lines I slowly trace
  Across this spotless page
Will time all earthly things efface
  And passing leave behind no trace
But the vile dusts of age;
  But truth and virtue mounting high
Shall heavenward wing their flight,
  And shine forever from the sky
Beyond the gems of night.

As jewels incased in a casket of gold,
  Where the richest of treasure we hide,
So our purest of thoughts lie deep and untold,
  Like the gems that are under the tide.

See Proverbs—4 Chap., 18, 19 Verses.
   Then choose at once,
    May the Lord guide thee.

There's little in earth's pomp and pride
  To lean on or to trust;
The wealth of earth cannot abide,
  It crumbles into dust.
But there'll remain, when other wealth
  Shall vanish and depart,
Far better than our sordid self—
  The love of one true heart.

  Every young man is now a sower of seed on the field of life. The bright days of youth are the seed-time. Every thought of your intellect, every emotion of your heart, every word of your tongue, every principle you adopt, every act you perform, is a seed whose good or evil fruit will prove bliss or bane of your after life.

Life is a leaf of paper white,
Whereon each one of us may write
His word or two, and then comes night.
Greatly begin! Though thou have time
But for a line, be that sublime;
Not failure, but low aim, is crime.

The fruits of a well spent life
Brings contentment and peace in old age—
Faithful to thy trust, duties well performed
Keep away the rust and drives back the storm.

Keep thy spirit pure, promptly do thy part,
God will surely bless and purify thy heart.

Little deeds of kindness, done in a quiet way,
Reach both deep and wide, and always bring their pay.

May'st thou live in joy forever,
Naught from thee true pleasure sever;
From thy heart arise no sigh,
And no tear bedew thine eye:
Joys be many, cares be few,
Smoothe the path thou shalt pursue,
And heaven's richest blessings shine
Ever on both thee and thine.

Guard well thy thoughts; our thoughts are heard in heaven.

As a slight token of esteem,
  Accept these lines from me;
So plain and simple, they do seem
  Unworthy such as thee.
But soon these traced lines will fade
  And disappear—'tis their doom.
May you, unlike them, be arrayed
  In a perpetual bloom.

Doubt thou the stars are fire;
  Doubt that the sun doth move;
Doubt Truth to be a liar;
  But never doubt I love!

Oh! how the passions, insolent and
    strong,
Bear our weak minds their rapid course
    along;
Make us the madness of their will
    obey;
Then die, and leave us to our griefs a
    prey.

There is a comfort in the strength of
    Love;
'Twill make a thing endurable, which
    else
Would overset the brain or break the
    heart.

I have heard of reasons manifold
  Why love must needs be blind;
But this the best of all I hold—
  His eyes are in his mind.
What outward form and feature are
  He guesseth but in part;
But what within is good and fair
  He seeeth with his heart.

Thou art beautiful, young lady—
  But I need not tell you this;
For few have borne, unconsciously,
  The spell of loveliness.

Oh fairest of creation! last and best
Of all God's works! creatures in whom
    excelled;
Whatever can to sight or thought be
    form'd
Holy, divine, good, amiable or sweet!

Love! What a volume in a word! an
    ocean in a tear!
A seventh heaven in a glance! a whirl-
    wind in a sigh!
The lightning in a touch—a millenium
    in a moment!
What concentrated joy, or woe, in blest
    or blighted love!

Farewell, oh farewell, but whenever you give
  A thought to the days that are gone,
Of the bright sunny things that in memory live,
  Let a thought of the writer be one.

Ye flowers that droop, forsaken by the spring;
Ye birds that, forsaken by the summer, cease to sing;
Ye trees that fade when autumn heats remove,
Say, is not absence death to those who love?

There are ten thousand tones and signs
We hear and see, but none defines—
Involuntary sparks of thought
Which strike from out the heart o'erwrought,
And form a strange intelligence
Alike mysterious and intense;
Which link the burning chain that binds,
Without their will, young hearts and minds,
Conveying as the electric wire,
We know not how, the absorbing fire.

Write your name in Love, Kindness and Charity, on the hearts of the people you come in contact with, and you will be loved by all.

When Time was entwining the garland
    of years,
 .Which to crown my beloved was
    given,
Though some of the leaves might be
    sullied with tears,
    Yet the flowers were all gathered in
    heaven.
And long may this garland be sweet to
    the eye,
    May its verdure forever be new!
Young Love shall enrich it with many
    a sigh,
    And Pity shall nurse it with dew.

Some friends may wish thee happiness,
    Some others wish thee wealth ;
My wish for thee is better far—
    Contentment, blest with health.

Let the road be rough and dreary,
    And its end far out of sight ;
Foot it bravely—strong or weary—
    Trust in God, and do the right.

Through time we'll change, and then
  This little book will somewhat bind
    us.
You'll take it up, and think of me
  And all the joys we've left behind us.

Live well; how long or short, permit
    to Heaven;
They who forgive most shall be most
    forgiven.

Our lives are albums; each new day's
    a page
  As spotless as the leaf on which I
    write.
Whene'er those books of ours shall be
    read,
  May few unwise inscriptions meet
    the sight.

Beauty is but a vain, a fleeting good,
  A shining gloss that fadeth suddenly,
A flower that dies when almost in the
    bud,
  A bright glass that breaketh suddenly;
A fleeting good, a glass, a gloss, a
    flower,
  Lost, faded, broken, dead within the
    hour.

Not purple violets in the early spring
Such graceful sweets, such tender
    beauties bring;
The orient blush which does thy cheeks
    adorn,
Makes coral pale—vies with the rosy
    morn.

Accomplishments are native to her
    mind,
  Like precious pearls within a clasp-
    ing shell,
And winning grace her every act re-
    fined,
  Like sunshine, shedding beauty where
    it fell.

The time is swiftly passing by
  When we must bid adieu.
We know not when we meet again,
  So these lines I leave with you.

There is pleasure in the pathless woods:
  There is rapture on the lonely shore;
There is society where none intrudes,
  By the deep sea, and music in its
    roar;
I love not man the less but nature
    more.

When the golden sun is sinking,
    And your mind from care and
        trouble's free;
When of others you are thinking,
    Won't you sometimes think of me?

A gentle word is never lost,
    Oh! never, then refuse one;
It cheers the heart when tempest-tossed,
    And lulls the cares that bruise one;
It scatters sunshine o'er our way,
    And turns our thorns to roses;
It changes weary night and day,
    And hope and love discloses.

If ever a husband you should have,
And he this book should see,
Tell him of your youthful days,
And kiss him once for me.

As o'er the cold sepulchral stone
    Some name arrests the passer-by,
Thus, when thou view'st this page alone,
    May mine attract thy pensive eye!

And when by thee that name is read,
    Perchance in some succeeding year,
Reflect on me as on the dead,
    And think my heart is buried here.

Save thy toiling, spare thy treasure,
All I ask is friendship's pleasure;
Let the shining orb lie darkling,
Bring no gem in lustre sparkling.
    Gifts and gold are naught to me;
    I would only look on thee!

Accept, my friend, these lines from me,
They show that I remember thee,
And hope some thought they will retain,
Till you and I shall meet again.

May Future, with her kindest smile,
    Wreath laurels for thy brow;
May loving angels guard and keep thee
    Ever pure as thou art now.

Count not the hours while their silent wings
    Thus waft them in fairy flight;
For feeling, warm from her dearest springs,
    Shall hallow the scene to-night.
And while the music of joy is here,
    And the colors of life are gay,
Let us think on those that have loved us dear—
    The friends who are far away.

In the evening of life cherish the remembrance of those who loved thee in its morning.

This album's a mansion which offers its best,
    To the friends who have written their thoughts,
And the banquet is spread with festal face,
    Where guests mingle enjoyment with rest;
And they leave their memorials under thy roof,
    Sometimes in sorrow, more oft in joy divine,
Nor think a single thought quite good enough,
    To measure its faintest pulse with thine.

Though many friends have signed their names,
    And some have left their mark,
I see a place for me remains
    To add my small remark.
My wish for thee is: joy through life;
    And bliss supreme, when some one's wife.

Here is one leaf reserved for me,
From all thy sweet memorials free;
And here my simple song might tell
The feelings thou must guess so well.
But could I thus within my mind
One little vacant corner find,
Where no impression yet is seen,
Where no memorial yet has been;
Oh, it should be my sweetest care
To write my name forever there!

   There is nothing but death
     Our affections can sever,
   And till life's latest breath
     Love shall bind us forever.

To write in your album, dear friend,
   you ask,
Ah, well! it is not such a difficult task.
All I can say is contained in one line
   here;
May the blessings of Heaven forever
   be thine.

A place in thy memory, dearest,
   Is all that I claim;
To pause and look back when thou
   hearest
     The sound of my name.

Let us be kind to each other!
   The night's coming on,
When friend and when brother
   Perchance may be gone!
Then, midst our dejection,
   How sweet to have earned
The blest recollection
   Of kindness returned.

I know not what to write about,
   So many themes are pressing;
All good enough in very truth,
   But quite unprepossessing:
Each moment of thy future life,
Live holy, whether maid or wife.

Fond Memory, come and hover o'er
   This album page of my dear friend;
Enrich her from thy precious store,
   And happy recollection send.
If on this page she chance to gaze,
   In years to come—where'er she be—
Tell her of earlier happy days,
   And bring her back one thought of
     me.

ESTEEM AND CONFIDENCE.

Some little token of regard,
   You wish from me to claim;
But as time is pressing hard,
   I will but write my name.

Every joy that heaven can send;
   Wealth, and every kind of treasure—
Health and love to thee, my friend,
   And happiness without measure.

In future years should trusted friends
   Depart like summer birds;
And all the comfort memory lends,
   Is false and honeyed words,
Turn then to me who fain would prove,
   However thy lot be cast,
That naught his heart can ever move
   From friendship of the past.

Speak of me kindly when life's dreams
     are o'er;
Speak of me gently when I am no
     more.

In the evening of life cherish the remembrance of one who loved thee in its morning.

Safely down Life's ebbing tide,
May our vessels smoothly glide,
And anchor side by side—in heaven.

That Hope and you,
Bright days will view.

May He who hath penciled the leaves with beauty, given the flowers their bloom, and lent music to the lay of the timid bird, graciously remember thee in that day when He shall gather His jewels.

To write in your Album, dear friend,
    you ask;
Ah, well! it is not such a difficult task.
All I can say is contained here in one
    line:
May the blessings of Heaven forever
    be thine.

A long life, and a happy one;
A tall man, and a jolly one—
Like—well—you know who!

May your path be strewn with roses,
  Fair and flowery to the end;
And when your body in death reposes,
  May your Maker be your friend.

Well, ———, I surely would like to
    please;
  But can't think what to say.
All your friends have wishes bright,
  To cheer your life so gay.

I will add: May all their words
  Be symbols of love and truth;
That when you grow weary, and seek
    for rest,
  You will rejoice in the friends of
    your youth.

The hills are shadows, and they flow
  From form to form, and nothing
    stands;
They melt like mist the solid lands,
  Like clouds they shape themselves
    and go.

But in my spirit will I dwell,
  And dream my dream and hold it
    true;
For though my pen doth write adieu,
  I cannot say for aye farewell.

God's love and peace be with thee, when
Soe'r this soft Autumnal air
Lifts the dark tresses of thy hair.

Thou lack'st not friendship's spellword, nor
The half-unconscious power to draw
All hearts to thine by Love's sweet law.

With such a prayer, on this sweet day,
As thou may'st hear and I may say,
I greet thee, dearest, far away.

———

This Album's a mansion which offers its best,
   To the friends who have written their thoughts,
And the banquet is spread with festal fare,
   Where guests mingle enjoyment with rest;
And they leave their memorials under thy roof,
   Sometimes in sorrow, more oft in joy divine,
Nor think a single thought quite good enough,
   To measure its faintest pulse with thine.

From memory's leaves,
I fondly squeeze
Three little words—
Forget Me Not.

Let not your friendship be like the rose, to sever;
But, like the evergreen, may it last forever.

He who does good to another does also good to himself—not only in the act, but in the consciousness of well-doing is his reward.

HUMOROUS.

I dip my pen into the ink,
    And grasp your album tight;
But for my life I cannot think
    One single word to write.

In the storms of life,
    When you need an umbrella,
May you have to uphold it
    A handsome young fellow.

    May beauty and truth,
        Keep you in youth;
    Green tea and sage,
        Preserve your old age.

Withsoever is this for why?
Wherefore.   Ain't it?

Round went the book, and here it came,
In it for me to write my name;
I would write better, if I could,
But nature said I never should.

Some people can be very funny,
  I never could be so.
So I'll just inscribe my name;
  It's the funniest thing I know.

Sailing down the stream of life,
  In your little bark canoe,
May you have a pleasant trip,
  With just room enough for two.

Dear Friend:
  Do not doubt me;
  You know more about me
  Than many whose names
      Here appear.

  But to tell them I'll never—
  What! never? Hardly ever—
  What I'd like to write to you
      Here.

  'Tis nonsense I've written;
  You'll think I am smitten
  With charms that I hold
      Very dear.

  Please excuse me from writing,
  More lines so inviting,
  Your time to be spent
      Idly here.

May your cheeks retain their dimples,
  May your heart be just as gay,
Until some manly voice shall whisper,
  "Dearest, will you name the day?"

I care not much for gold or land,
  Give me a mortgage here and there,
Some good bank stock—some note of hand,
  Or trifling railroad share,
I only ask that Fortune send
  A little more than I can spend.

Fee simple and simple fee,
  And all the fees entail
Are nothing when compared to thee—
  Thou best of fees—fe-male.

What! write in your album, for critics to spy,
For the learned to laugh at?—No, not I!

  Accept my valued friendship,
    And roll it up in cotton,
  And think it not illusion,
    Because so easily gotten.

When on this page you chance to look,
Think of me and close the book.

If you wish to laugh,
Glance at my autograph.

Man's love is like Scotch snuff—
You take a pinch and that's enough.
Profit by this sage advice,
When you fall in love, think twice.

Long may you live,
Happy may you be,
When you get married
Come and see me.

May you be happy,
Each day of your life.
Get a good husband
And make a good wife.

As sure as comes your wedding day,
A broom to you I'll send;
In *sunshine*, use the brushy part,
In *storm*, the other end.

I write in your Album?
How very absurd!
My mind is at random—

BIRTHDAY VERSES.

Your Birthday will always be green in the memory of your friends.

May these flowers, presented on your birthday, be emblematical of the purity of your life.

Wake early this morning,
Nor miss the grey dawning;
Take this greeting from me
As it goes straight to thee:
May joy and gladness e'er be thine;
And endless brightness round thee shine.

Like sunbeams to the drooping flowers,
   Good-will our lives doth bless;
It furthers every wish of ours,
   And joys in our success.
So may its rays towards you flow,
   That none but friends your heart may know.

I wish thee every blessing
  That can attend thee here;
And may each future birthday prove
  My wish to be sincere.

In these days of mirth and glee,
What shall my message be to thee?
What can I wish for one so blest?
Thou sunny bird in a sunny nest!
This I wish, and this I pray:
May the joys of life never pass away,
But only merge in a sigh of bliss—
Into a life far brighter than this!

If words could all my wishes say,
Oh! how my tongue would talk away.
I wish this day and many more
Might on dear ——— blessings pour.
May health, wealth, love, and peace
With each succeeding year increase;
And oh! the last, come when it may,
Be unto thee a happy day.

As beauteous flowers in garlands inter-
    twine,
May Peace and Love to cheer thy heart
    combine,
  To give you a very happy Birthday,

This is thy Birthday, may it be,
A source of happiness to thee,
And may each Birthday yet in store,
Be brighter than the one before.

———

Dear friend, on this, thy natal day,
I send to thee a little lay,
                    And wishes tender
And only ask that thou'lt repay
My thoughts with thine, and fondly say,
                 "I thank the sender."

May Spring its blossoms round thee strew,
And Summer, deck'd in mantle new,
                   Come forth to greet thee ;
May Autumn fruitage crown the year,
And Winter, with its jovial cheer,
                   Bring friends to meet thee.

And if I still must absent be,
Do not forget to send to me
                   One kind word only,
By home birds passing by the door,
Who, flying towards this distant shore,
                   May greet me lonely.

CHRISTMAS AND NEW-YEAR VERSES.

Joy and plenty in the cottage,
  Peace and feasting in the hall;
And the voices of the children
  Ring out clear above it all:
    A merry Christmas!

  Health and prosperity
    Your life to cheer,
  With every blessing
    For the bright New Year.

Ring out, ye bells, o'er all the earth,
  To tell with brazen voice,
The tidings of the Saviour's birth
  And bid mankind rejoice.

Hark, the pearly air is trembling,
  Liquid music floats along;
Angels, in sweet joy assembling,
  Thrill the skies with heavenly song.
"Peace on Earth," is their refrain,
  Oh! be it yours this peace to gain.

On this New Year's morning
　My wishes take their flight,
And wing to thee a greeting
　That would make all things bright.

O, life is but a river
　And in our childhood we,
But a fair and running streamlet
　Adorned with flowers, see.

But as we grow more earnest,
　The river grows more deep,
And where we laughed in childhood,
　We, older, pause to weep.

Each Christmas, as it passes,
　Some change to us doth bring,
Yet to our friends the closer,
　As time creeps on, we cling.

Gladly now it is my pleasure,
Joys to wish you, without measure,
Happiness and peace attending,
With pure heavenly blessings blending.

True love shall live thro' sorrow's wintry storm,
And bloom afresh on this glad Christmas morn.

For friends we strive to pierce
  The future, dense and dark,
But not a ray of light
  We see, nor faintest spark;
But yet while we have faith to cheer,
We trusting wish " A bright New Year."

May piety with wishes placed above,
And steady loyalty and faithful love,
Be thy blessings this Christmas-tide.

May health and joy, and peace be thine
  Upon this Christmas day,
And happy faces round thee shine
  As plenteous as the flowers in May.

Now Christmas comes with hearty
    cheer,
  May kindly thoughts go round,
And bring to you a glad New Year,
  With peace and plenty crowned.

Christmas is coming, and what will it
    bring?
Many a pleasant and gladdening thing!
Meetings and greetings, and innocent
    mirth:
All that is brightest and best on the
    earth.

A little bird comes singing,
   Singing a song to you;
He sings of sun-tipped flowers,
   Bathed in a diamond dew.
"The days are coming," he warbles,
   "When the frost has flown away,
When the earth will be sweet with
     flowers
   And the breath of new-mown hay."

Oh bird so softly singing
   Your song of pleasant days,
Go sing to her I fondly love,
   Through the wintry cold and bare.
When the heart is light, the days are
     bright,
   And the sun seems ever near;
So sing her your lay this Christmas Day,
   And through all the bright New Year.

Ring in, ring in the revelries,
   And let the feast be one
Where not a single guest there is
   But Innocence and Fun!
Let Christmas warmth keep winter out,
   And joy unbroken reign—
From floor to rooftree send the shout
   Till Christmas comes again!

Christmas comes, let every heart
In Christmas customs bear its part:
The "old" be "young," the sad be gay,
And smiles chase every care away.

Our Saviour Christ was born
That we might have the Rose without
    the thorn,
  All through His desert life
  He felt the thorns of human sin and
    strife.
His blessed feet were bare
To every hurting brier. He did not
    spare
  One bleeding footstep on the way
  He came to trace for us, until the day
The cruel crown was pressed upon the
    Brow
That smiles upon us from His glory
    now.
And so He won for us
Sweet, thornless, everlasting flowers
    thus.
  He bids our desert way
  Rejoice and blossom as the Rose to-
    day.
There is no hidden thorn
In His good gifts of grace. He would
    adorn

The lives that now are His alone,
With brightness and beauty all his own.
Then praise the Lord who came on Christmas day
To give the Rose and take the thorns away.

I cannot tell what thou wilt bring to me,
O strange New Year,
But tho' thick darkness shrouds thy days and months,
I will not fear.
Why should I fret my heart to know before
What may befall?
With this one thought content—I ask no more—
God knows it all.

Again the festive season's here,
With all that can delight and cheer;
Oh! may you nothing lack each day,
But find fresh blessings strew your way.

Take, my friend, this heartfelt greeting,
Happy be thy Christmas day,
Faith, and hope, and love here meeting,
Speed thee on thy New Year's way!

Sure, Christmas is a happy time
　In spite of wintry weather,
For laugh, and song, and jest go round
　When dear friends meet together;
And hearts are warm, and eyes beam
　　bright
In the ruddy glow of Christmas night!

———

As Christmas offerings meet your eyes,
Still closer be sweet friendship's ties.

———

Oh joyous be your Chistmas-tide,
　And bright your New Year, too;
To you may love ne'er be denied;
　May all your friends be true.

———

Oh! may thy Christmas happy be,
　And naught but joy appear,
Is now the wish I send to thee,
　And all I love most dear.

———

O bright be the day
　Sweet echoes resounding,
Love lighting the way
　And warm hearts surrounding.
May the breath of His peace
　In thy spirit remain,
Till Christmas revisits
　The round world again!

O childhood is a golden time,
  When all the world is bright,
When sunshine comes with every morn,
  Sweet dreams with every night.
Were I a fairy, I would give
  To thee a magic kiss,
That should ensure for the New Year,
  As fair a time as this.

A BAD BOY'S DIARY.

This is the most humorous book ever issued from the Press. The *One Hundreth Thousand* has just been issued, and the demand for it is still increasing. One editor says of it: "It made us laugh till our sides ached and the tears came." Another says: "It will drive the blues out of a bag of indigo. It is worth a dollar, but costs only ten cents." One reader says of it: "I received the Bad Boy's Diary you sent me, and as most of my family are killed by laughing over it, you may send another copy, so I can dispose of the rest of them in the same happy manner."

It contains 48 pages and is handsomely illustrated. Sent by mail on receipt of Ten Cents.

DIARY OF A MINISTER'S WIFE.

"It excels Mark Twain for genuine humor."

This is one of the most humorous books of the present day, showing in a manner pleasing to all readers the trials, tribulations, expectations, and actual experiences of a "minister's wife" in a country parish. The characters represented are true to life, and will doubtless bring to the mind of the reader remembrances of events and individuals within their own knowledge. It contains 64 pages, with handsome engraved cover. Price Ten Cents.

"A BUSHEL OF FUN,"

gathered from the writings of authors of "A Bad Boy's Diary," Josh Billings, Detroit Free Press Man, Burlington Hawkeye Man, Max Adeler, and other funny men and women.

This is, indeed, a whole bushel of funny things, well shaken down, and running over with fun and good humor. It contains 64 pages, and is handsomely illustrated. Price Ten Cents.

☞ The above books are for sale by Newsdealers and Booksellers. Either of them will be mailed on receipt of price by the Publishers,

Address, **J. S. OGILVIE & CO., Publishers**
  31 Rose Street, New York.

www.ingramcontent.com/pod-product-compliance
Lightning Source LLC
Chambersburg PA
CBHW022138160426
43197CB00009B/1336